MASTER MEME TRADING

REAL WORLD GUIDE TO SUCCESS IN THE CRYPTO MARKET

Corey Ruffin

Copyright © 2024 by Corey Ruffin

All rights reserved.

No portion of this book may be reproduced in any form without written permission from the publisher or author, except as permitted by U.S. copyright law.

This publication is designed to provide accurate and authoritative information in regard to the subject matter covered. It is sold with the understanding that neither the author nor the publisher is engaged in rendering legal, investment, accounting or other professional services. While the publisher and author have used their best efforts in preparing this book, they make no representations or warranties with respect to the accuracy or completeness of the contents of this book and specifically disclaim any implied warranties of merchantability or fitness for a particular purpose.

No warranty may be created or extended by sales representatives or written sales materials. The advice and strategies contained herein may not be suitable for your situation. You should consult with a professional when appropriate.

Neither the publisher nor the author shall be liable for any loss of profit or any other commercial damages, including but not limited to special, incidental, consequential, personal, or other damages.

Cover Art by Corey Ruffin

1st edition 2024

This book is dedicated to my mother, Peggy who from day one told me to shoot for the moon!

In the precious name of Yahusha,
I Love you Ma!

PREFACE

In the vast and ever-evolving landscape of cryptocurrency, where innovation and speculation intertwine, a new phenomenon has emerged, the meme coin. Born from the depths of internet culture, these digital tokens have captured the attention of traders and investors worldwide with their whimsical names, charismatic mascots, and seemingly boundless potential for explosive growth.

But within a seemingly chaotic world lies a hidden gem that start with mastering meme coin trading. It is a skill that requires equal parts intuition, strategy, and risk management. As the popularity of meme coins continues to soar, so too does the need for a comprehensive guide to navigate this unpredictable market.

In this book, we embark on a journey to uncover the secrets of trading all markets! In particular meme coin trading. From understanding the fundamentals of blockchain technology to deciphering the psychology behind viral memes, we delve deep into the forces that drive these digital currencies to astronomical heights or plummeting lows.

Through real-world examples, expert insights, and practical strategies, we will equip you with the knowledge and tools necessary to navigate the turbulent waters of meme coin trading. Whether you're a seasoned cryptocurrency investor or a curious newcomer, this book will serve as your compass in the wild frontier of meme coin madness.

Lets embark on a quest to master the art of meme coin trading and unlock the potential for untold riches in this electrifying new frontier of finance.

CONTENTS

Copyright
Dedication
Preface

1.	The Rise of Meme Coins	7
2.	Understanding Blockchain Basics	11
3.	Deciphering Meme Coin Economics	14
4.	The Psychology of Memes and Markets	18
5.	Identifying Meme Coin Opportunities	22
6.	Navigating Meme Coin Exchanges	27
7.	Risk Management in Meme Coin Trading	31
8.	Riding the Meme Coin Waves	35
9.	The Dark Side of Meme Coin Trading	39
10.	Mastering Meme Coin Trading	44
11.	Dispelling the Myth of "To the Moon"	47
12.	Trading Strategies	49
13.	Trading Terms	52
14.	Putting it All Together	56
15.	Notes Pages	70
16.	Conclusion	78
17.	Glossary	79

CHAPTER 1

THE RISE OF MEME COINS

Image used solely for illustration

From Doge to Shib!

The history of meme coins, from Dogecoin to Shiba Inu, is a fascinating journey that intertwines with internet culture, community-driven initiatives, and the ever-evolving landscape of cryptocurrency. Let's delve into the origins and evolution of meme.

Dogecoin - The OG Meme Coin

Dogecoin emerged in December 2013 as a playful and lighthearted cryptocurrency inspired by the popular "Doge" meme, featuring a Shiba Inu dog.

Created by software engineers Billy Markus and Jackson Palmer, Dogecoin was initially intended as a joke or parody of the booming cryptocurrency scene at the time. However, its welcoming and meme-centric community quickly propelled it to prominence. One of the defining features of Dogecoin was its strong community spirit and commitment to charitable causes. Dogecoin enthusiasts often engaged in fundraising efforts, donating to various charitable organizations and sponsoring events. This ethos of generosity and inclusivity endeared Dogecoin to many, further fueling its popularity.

Impact on Internet Culture

Dogecoin's success not only demonstrated the power of internet memes but also highlighted the influence of online communities in shaping digital currencies. Its meme-centric branding and grassroots marketing efforts resonated with a younger demographic, attracting newcomers to the world of cryptocurrency.

Following Dogecoin's success, numerous other meme coins began to emerge, often inspired by internet memes or cultural references. While many of these coins started as jokes or experiments, some gained significant traction and market value. Newer meme coins like PepeCoin, Bonk, Garlicoin, and others have since garnered attention, albeit to a lesser extent than Dogecoin.

Shiba Inu Coin - Riding the Meme Wave

Shiba Inu Coin (SHIB) emerged onto the cryptocurrency scene in August 2020, drawing inspiration from the success of Dogecoin (DOGE) and embracing the same Shiba Inu dog meme theme. Positioned as the "Dogecoin Killer," SHIB sought to ride the wave of enthusiasm

Images used solely for illustrative purpose only!

surrounding meme coins and capitalize on the burgeoning interest in decentralized finance (DeFi) and non-fungible tokens (NFTs).

One of the key factors contributing to SHIB's rapid rise in popularity was its decentralized community and meme-centric branding. Similar to Dogecoin, SHIB fostered a vibrant and active community of supporters, known as the "ShibArmy," who enthusiastically promoted the coin across social media platforms and online forums. This grassroots movement played a significant role in driving awareness and adoption of SHIB among cryptocurrency enthusiasts and retail investors.

Moreover, SHIB differentiated itself from other meme coins by introducing innovative tokenomics and utility features. For instance, SHIB operates on the Ethereum blockchain and leverages smart contracts to implement deflationary mechanisms, such as token burning and liquidity locking, to increase scarcity and value over time. Additionally, SHIB introduced the concept of decentralized autonomous organization (DAO) governance, allowing token holders to participate in decision-making processes and community-driven initiatives.

Furthermore, SHIB's ecosystem expanded to include a range of decentralized applications (dApps) and partnerships within the DeFi and NFT sectors. These initiatives aimed to enhance the utility and functionality of SHIB tokens, offering users opportunities to stake, yield farm, and participate in NFT marketplaces built on the SHIB ecosystem.

Disruption in the Cryptocurrency Market

Meme coins like Dogecoin and Shiba Inu have disrupted the cryptocurrency market in several ways. They've challenged traditional notions of value and utility, highlighting the role of community sentiment and social media influence in driving asset prices. Moreover, their rapid rise in popularity has forced industry observers to reassess the dynamics of digital asset valuation and investment behavior.

However, meme coins are often characterized by high levels of speculation and volatility. Their prices can experience dramatic fluctuations based on social media trends, celebrity endorsements, and market sentiment. While some investors have profited from meme coins' meteoric rises, others have faced substantial losses due to their unpredictable nature.

In summary, meme coins like Dogecoin and Shiba Inu have played a significant role in shaping internet culture and disrupting the cryptocurrency market. Their meme-centric branding, community-driven ethos, and speculative appeal have attracted widespread attention, challenging traditional notions of value and investment. As the crypto landscape continues to evolve, meme coins are likely to remain a prominent and intriguing phenomenon, reflecting the dynamic interplay between technology, culture, and finance.

CHAPTER 2

UNDERSTANDING BLOCKCHAIN BASICS

Building Blocks of the Future

In the realm of cryptocurrencies like Doge and Shib, blockchain technology serves as the underlying infrastructure that enables their existence and operation. To comprehend meme coins fully, it's essential to grasp the foundational concepts of blockchain. Let's explore the key components and principles of blockchain technology.

What is Blockchain?

At its core, a blockchain is a decentralized, distributed ledger that records transactions across a network of computers. Each block in the chain contains a set of transactions, and these blocks are linked together in chronological order, forming a continuous chain.

Unlike traditional centralized systems controlled by a single entity (e.g., banks or governments), blockchain operates in a decentralized manner. This means that no single authority has control over the network. Instead, the network is maintained by a distributed network of nodes, each containing a copy of the blockchain.

Transactions recorded on a blockchain are transparent and immutable, meaning they cannot be altered or deleted once they are added to the ledger. This feature ensures the integrity and trustworthiness of the data stored on the blockchain, as anyone can verify the transaction history.

Consensus mechanisms are protocols that ensure all nodes in the network agree on the validity of transactions and the order in which they are added to the blockchain. Popular consensus mechanisms include Proof of Work (PoW), used by Bitcoin, and Proof of Stake (PoS), used by Ethereum. These mechanisms incentivize network participants to validate transactions and maintain the integrity of the blockchain.

Cryptography plays a crucial role in securing the blockchain by encrypting transaction data and providing privacy and authentication mechanisms. Each transaction is cryptographically signed by the sender, ensuring that only the intended recipient can access the funds.

Smart contracts are self-executing contracts with the terms of the agreement directly written into code.

They enable automated and trustless transactions, allowing parties to interact with each other without the need for intermediaries. Smart contracts are a feature of certain blockchain platforms like Ethereum.

Blockchains can be categorized as public or private. Public blockchains, like Bitcoin and Ethereum, are open to anyone to join and participate in the network. Private blockchains, on the other hand, are permission only networks where access is restricted to authorized participants.

Understanding these foundational concepts of blockchain technology provides insights into how meme coins operate within this decentralized ecosystem. Meme coins leverage blockchain's transparency, decentralization, and consensus mechanisms to enable peer-to-peer transactions and foster community-driven initiatives. By embracing the principles of blockchain, meme coins have carved out a niche in the ever-evolving landscape of digital currencies, showcasing the transformative potential of decentralized technologies.

CHAPTER 3

DECIPHERING MEME COIN ECONOMICS

The Value of Laughter

Meme coin economics encompasses a unique set of factors that drive their valuation within the cryptocurrency market. While meme coins share some similarities with traditional cryptocurrencies, such as Bitcoin and Ethereum, their valuation is often influenced by distinct dynamics shaped by internet culture, community sentiment, and viral trends.

Supply and Demand Dynamics

Like any other asset, meme coin valuation is subject to the fundamental forces of supply and demand. The total supply of a meme coin, often determined by its initial token distribution and issuance schedule, plays a crucial role in shaping its scarcity and perceived value. Scarcity can create a sense of exclusivity and drive up demand, leading to price appreciation.

Demand for meme coins is heavily influenced by various factors, including community engagement, social media trends, celebrity endorsements, and speculative hype. Meme coins that garner widespread attention and adoption within online communities often experience surges in demand, resulting in price rallies.

Conversely, excessive token supply or lack of community interest can lead to oversupply and diminished demand, causing meme coin prices to stagnate or decline.

Liquidity

Liquidity refers to the ease with which meme coins can be bought or sold without significantly impacting their market price. High liquidity is essential for ensuring price stability and facilitating efficient trading within cryptocurrency exchanges.

Meme coins with strong liquidity benefit from active trading volumes and robust order books, allowing investors to enter and exit positions with minimal slippage. On the other hand, illiquid meme coins may experience sharp price fluctuations and limited trading opportunities, making them riskier assets to trade.

ill·li·quid
/ˌilˈliˌqid/
Illiquid refers to the state of a stock, bond, or other assets that cannot easily and readily be sold or exchanged for cash without a substantial loss

Factors influencing liquidity include exchange support, trading volume, market depth, and token distribution among investors. Projects that prioritize liquidity initiatives, such as liquidity mining programs or partnerships with decentralized exchanges (DEXs), can enhance the liquidity profile of their meme coins.

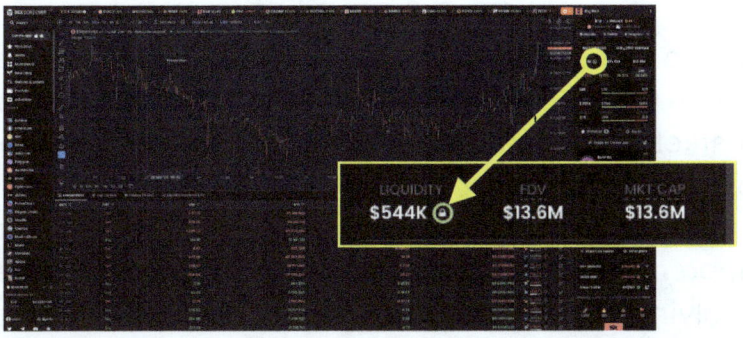

TIPS & TECHNIQUES

Programs such as Dex Screener allow users to not only see the crypto assets liquidity but also shows if this liquidity is locked or not.

Dex Screener is a powerful and free cryptocurrency analysis and screening tool that allows crypto investors to analyze assets across multiple decentralized exchanges (DEXs) and networks.

Market Sentiment

Market sentiment plays a significant role in shaping meme coin valuation, often driving short-term price movements and investor behavior. Unlike traditional financial markets, sentiment within the cryptocurrency space is highly influenced by social media platforms, online forums, and community-driven narratives.

Positive sentiment surrounding a meme coin, fueled by viral memes, positive news coverage, or community excitement, can create a self-reinforcing cycle of buying activity and price appreciation. Conversely, negative sentiment stemming from controversies, regulatory scrutiny, or community disillusionment can trigger sell-offs and price declines.

Meme coins with strong community support and active social media engagement tend to exhibit more resilient market sentiment, as loyal supporters rally behind the project during periods of volatility. However, sentiment-driven price movements can be highly unpredictable and subject to rapid shifts based on evolving narratives and external events.

In summary, meme coin economics is shaped by a complex interplay of supply and demand dynamics, liquidity considerations, and market sentiment. Understanding these economic principles is essential for navigating the volatile world of meme coin trading and making informed investment decisions.

CHAPTER 4

THE PSYCHOLOGY OF MEMES AND MARKETS

From LOL to ROI...

Memes are more than just humorous images or catchy phrases shared across the internet; they are powerful cultural artifacts that tap into deep-seated psychological processes and social dynamics. Understanding the psychology behind memes is essential for comprehending their influence on investor behavior and market trends.

Memes often evoke strong emotional responses from individuals, ranging from laughter and amusement to surprise, nostalgia, or even outrage. These connections play a crucial role in how memes are perceived, shared, and remembered within online communities.

Images used solely for illustrative

$TD BIG   MARVIN $CULO   PEPE   KIMBO

In the context of meme coin trading, memes serve as vehicles for emotional engagement and community bonding among investors. Memes can create a sense of camaraderie and belonging among like-minded individuals, fostering a supportive community culture that reinforces positive sentiment and collective action.

Emotional attachment to memes can also influence investor decision-making, as individuals may be more inclined to invest in meme coins associated with familiar or beloved memes that evoke positive emotions.

Social Identity and Belonging

Memes often serve as cultural signifiers that signal membership within specific online communities or subcultures. By sharing and engaging with memes, individuals express their social identity and affiliation with particular groups, ideologies, or cultural references.

In the context of meme coin trading, the sense of belonging fostered by meme culture can drive investor participation and enthusiasm for meme coin projects. Investors may perceive meme coins as more than just financial assets; they represent symbols of community identity and shared values.

Social identity theory suggests that individuals are motivated to maintain a positive self-image and social status within their chosen communities. Consequently, investors may be more likely to support meme coins endorsed by influential community members or aligned with their group's norms and beliefs.

Virality and FOMO

vi·ral·i·ty
/ˌvīˈralədē/

The tendency of an image, video, or piece of information to be circulated rapidly and widely from one internet user to another; the quality or

Memes thrive on virality, spreading rapidly across social media platforms through networks of sharing and imitation. Memes that resonate with a broad audience or tap into current cultural trends are more likely to go viral, reaching millions of users within a short period.

In the context of meme coin trading, viral memes can fuel fear of missing out (FOMO) among investors, driving speculative buying activity and price rallies. Investors may fear being left behind as meme coins gain momentum and attract widespread attention, leading to impulsive investment decisions.

The fear of missing out on potential profits or social validation can override rational decision-making processes, contributing to market volatility and speculative bubbles within the meme coin ecosystem.

In summary, the psychology behind memes encompasses emotional connection, social identity, virality, and fear of missing out. These psychological factors influence investor behavior and market trends within meme coin trading, shaping the dynamics of community engagement, sentiment, and speculative activity. Understanding the interplay between memes and investor psychology is essential for navigating the unpredictable landscape of meme coin markets.

CHAPTER 5

IDENTIFYING MEME COIN OPPORTUNITIES

Uncovering Hidden Gems

Identifying promising meme coins requires a combination of research, due diligence, and risk assessment to separate potential winners from the vast array of projects flooding the cryptocurrency market. Here are some strategies to equip you with the tools necessary to identify meme coins with the potential for explosive growth.

You may have noticed the **"Tips & Techniques"** callout earlier in the Liquidity section in Ch.3 Look for them throughout. These are some of the exact steps I take and tools I use when analyzing potential trades.

- **Research Methodology**

Stay Informed: Keep abreast of the latest trends, news, and developments within the cryptocurrency and meme coin communities. Follow influential figures, forums, and social media channels where discussions about meme coins take place.

Note: There's a list of reputable sites for research, info, trading and community groups at the end of the book.

Explore Online Communities: Engage with online communities on X (fka Twitter) and forums dedicated to meme coins, such as Reddit's r/CryptoCurrency and r/MemeEconomy. Participate in discussions, ask questions, and observe community sentiment towards different projects.

> **TIP**
> When you find a group that interest you click on some of the top contributors and individuals who interact regularly within the group. See what other coins they are commenting on. This is a great way to discover new projects and opportunities!

Conduct Thorough Analysis: Evaluate meme coins based on factors such as project fundamentals, team credentials, technology, community engagement, and roadmap. Look for transparency, credibility, and innovation within project documentation and communications.

- **Due Diligence**

Assess Project Fundamentals: Evaluate the underlying fundamentals of meme coin projects, including their whitepapers, roadmaps, and tokenomics. Assess the project's goals, utility, governance structure, and long-term viability. All of this should be accessible on the projects website.

Images used solely for illustrative purpose only!

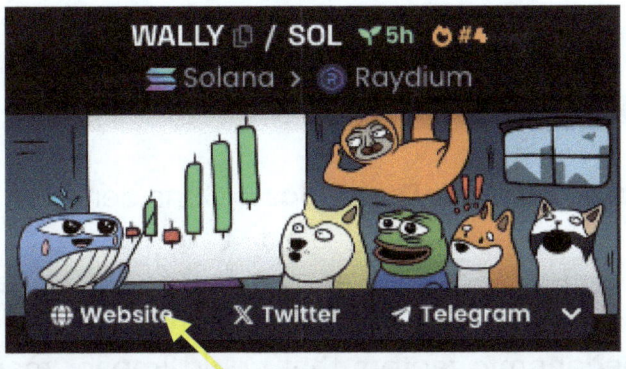

TIP
Dex Screener allows you to easily access a projects fundamental elements at the click of a button

Review Team Credentials: Research the backgrounds and expertise of the project's development team, advisors, and partners. Look for evidence of relevant experience, technical proficiency, and a track record of successful projects.

Analyze Technology: Evaluate the technological aspects of the meme coin, such as its blockchain platform, consensus mechanism, scalability, and security features. Assess whether the technology is robust, innovative, and capable of delivering on its promises.

Examine Community Engagement: Gauge the level of community engagement and support surrounding the meme coin project. Look for active communities on social media platforms, forums, and messaging channels, as well as the quality of interactions and discussions.

- **Risk Assessment**

Evaluate Market Dynamics: Consider the current market conditions and trends within the cryptocurrency space. Assess factors such as overall market sentiment, investor appetite for risk, and macroeconomic factors that could impact meme coin valuations. Like any other asset, macroeconomic factors impact investor sentiment, market dynamics, and the broader economy. Some of these factors are interest rates, inflation, regulations and economic growth to name a few.

Assess Regulatory Risks: Evaluate the regulatory environment surrounding meme coins and cryptocurrencies in general. As mentioned earlier, be aware of potential regulatory risks, legal challenges, and compliance requirements that could affect the project's operations and market acceptance.

Consider Financial Risks: Assess the financial risks associated with investing in meme coins, including volatility, liquidity, and market manipulation.

Be prepared for price fluctuations and potential losses, and only invest what you can afford to lose.

Diversify Your Portfolio: Mitigate risk by diversifying your meme coin investments across multiple projects and asset classes. Avoid putting all your eggs in one basket and spread your investments across different sectors, themes, and risk profiles.

By combining thorough research, due diligence, and risk assessment, you can identify meme coins with the potential for explosive growth while minimizing the risks associated with speculative investments in the cryptocurrency market.

Keep in mind that investing in meme coins like any other type of investing carries inherent risks, and it's essential to approach it with caution and a long-term perspective.

CHAPTER 6
NAVIGATING MEME COIN EXCHANGES

Trading in the Modern Wild West

Navigating meme coin exchanges requires careful consideration of factors such as platform reputation, security measures, trading fees, liquidity, and user experience. Here's a guide to help readers navigate the process of trading meme coins on various cryptocurrency exchanges.

Research and Selecting the Right Exchange

Research the reputation and track record of cryptocurrency exchanges offering meme coin trading. Look for exchanges with a history of reliability, security, and responsive customer support. Prioritize exchanges that implement robust security measures, such as two-factor authentication (2FA), cold storage of funds, and regular security audits. Avoid platforms with a history of security breaches or inadequate safeguards.

Note: There is a list of reputable sites at the end of the book

Supported Meme Coins: Check which meme coins are listed on the exchange and whether they offer sufficient trading pairs and liquidity for the coins you're interested in trading. Choose exchanges that support a diverse range of meme coins to maximize trading opportunities. Ensure that the exchange complies with relevant regulatory requirements and operates in jurisdictions with clear legal frameworks for cryptocurrency trading. Avoid platforms operating in jurisdictions with uncertain regulatory environments or legal risks.

Setting Up Your Trading Account

Complete the account verification process required by the exchange, which typically involves providing personal information and identity verification documents. Verify your account to unlock higher trading limits and access additional features. Enable security features such as two-factor authentication (2FA) and withdrawal whitelists to enhance the security of your trading account. Use strong, unique passwords and consider using a hardware wallet for storing funds offline.

Deposit funds into your exchange account using supported deposit methods, such as bank transfers, credit/debit cards, or cryptocurrency deposits. Be aware of deposit fees, processing times, and minimum deposit requirements imposed by the exchange.

Placing Trades and Managing Risks

Conduct thorough market analysis and research before placing trades. Monitor price charts, order books, and trading volume to identify trends, support/resistance levels, and potential entry/exit points.

Price / **MCap**   USD / SOL

> **TIP**
> Because Crypto Coin prices vary in such an extreme degree, I find it easier to set my charts to MARKET CAP vs PRICE. You will be amazed at the consistency in which these key spots are traded.

Familiarize yourself with different order types offered by the exchange, such as market orders, limit orders and stop-loss orders. Choose the appropriate order type based on your trading strategy and risk tolerance. Implement risk management strategies to mitigate potential losses and protect your investment capital. Set stop-loss orders to limit downside risk, diversify your portfolio and avoid investing more than you can afford to lose.

Also make sure you monitor Your Trades! Keep a close eye on your open trades and market conditions. Be prepared to adjust your trading strategy based on changing market dynamics, news events and price movements.

Withdrawal and Security:

Review the withdrawal process. When you're ready to withdraw funds from the exchange, ensure that you comply with the platform's withdrawal procedures and security protocols. Verify withdrawal addresses and double-check transaction details to avoid errors.

Secure Your Assets: Transfer your meme coins to a secure wallet for long-term storage, such as a hardware wallet or a reputable software wallet. Take precautions to safeguard your private keys and backup your wallet to prevent loss of funds.

By following these steps and tips, you should be able to navigate meme coin exchanges with confidence, select the right platform for your trading needs, and manage trading risks effectively in the dynamic world of cryptocurrency trading.

CHAPTER 7

RISK MANAGEMENT IN MEME COIN TRADING

The Balancing Act

Risk management is essential for meme coin traders to mitigate potential losses and protect their investments in the volatile cryptocurrency market. Here are some effective risk management strategies tailored specifically for meme coin trading.

Diversification!

Diversification involves spreading investments across multiple meme coins and asset classes to reduce overall portfolio risk. By diversifying, traders can mitigate the impact of adverse price movements in any single meme coin.

Allocate your investment capital across a diverse range of meme coins with varying levels of risk, liquidity, and growth potential. Avoid concentrating your investments in a single meme coin or relying too heavily on a few projects.

Some of the newer networks such as Solana, Polygon and Avalanche can be a great place to start. Because of there super low gas & transaction fees they have become very popular in the meme trading community.

Position Sizing

Position sizing involves determining the amount of capital to allocate to each meme coin trade based on risk tolerance and portfolio objectives. Avoid risking more than a predetermined percentage of your total capital on any single trade.

Calculate position sizes based on factors such as the size of your trading account, risk-reward ratio, and stop-loss levels. Adjust position sizes accordingly to align with your risk management strategy and account for market conditions.

Set Stop-Loss Orders

Implement stop-loss orders to automatically exit trades at predefined price levels to limit potential losses. Set stop-loss orders at strategic levels based on technical analysis, support/resistance zones, or percentage-based thresholds.

Determine stop-loss levels based on factors such as volatility, liquidity, and risk tolerance. Regularly review and adjust stop-loss orders as market conditions evolve to protect profits and minimize downward risk.

Use Take-Profit Targets

Set take-profit targets to lock in profits and exit trades at predetermined price levels. Take-profit targets should be based on realistic expectations of price movement and align with your trading strategy and risk-reward ratio.

Implement a systematic approach to setting take-profit targets, considering factors such as technical indicators, market sentiment, and fundamental analysis. Consider scaling out of positions gradually as price targets are reached to maximize profitability.

Manage Position Leverage

Exercise caution when trading meme coins with leverage, as amplified gains come with increased risk of losses. Avoid excessive leverage and use leverage levels that align with your risk tolerance and trading experience.

Monitor and manage leverage positions closely, ensuring adequate margin levels and maintaining sufficient account equity to withstand price fluctuations. Consider reducing leverage during periods of high volatility or uncertainty in the market.

Stay Informed and Adapt

Stay informed about market developments, news events, and emerging trends within the meme coin ecosystem. Continuously monitor market conditions and adjust your trading strategy and risk management approach accordingly. Remain flexible and adaptable in response to changing market dynamics, adjusting position sizes, stop-loss levels, and take-profit targets as needed.

Avoid becoming **emotionally** attached to trades and be prepared to cut losses quickly to preserve capital!

By implementing these risk management strategies, meme coin traders can navigate the volatile cryptocurrency market more effectively, mitigate potential losses, and protect their investments in meme coins. Remember that risk management is a continuous process that requires discipline, patience, and adaptability to succeed in meme coin trading.

CHAPTER 8

RIDING THE MEME COIN WAVES

Catching the Wave!

Riding meme coin momentum involves capitalizing on price fluctuations and market trends to maximize trading profits. Here are some strategies for meme coin traders to effectively ride momentum and seize opportunities for profit.

Trend Following

Trend following involves identifying and trading in the direction of established market trends. Monitor price charts and technical indicators to identify meme coins with strong upward momentum and bullish price patterns.

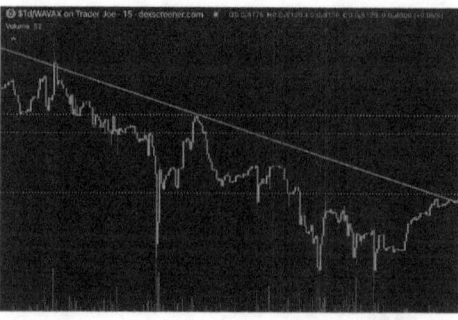

Just like other markets crypto follows trends often bouncing off past support and resistance levels.

Look for meme coins that are breaking out of consolidation patterns, forming higher highs and higher lows and exhibiting increasing trading volume. Enter trades when the trend is confirmed and ride the momentum until signs of trend exhaustion or reversal appear.

Breakout Trading

Breakout trading involves entering positions when meme coins break out of key levels of support or resistance, signaling potential shifts in market momentum. Monitor price action and volume to identify breakout opportunities.

Wait for confirmation of a breakout by observing price movement and volume expansion. Enter trades on breakout pullbacks or retracements to key support or resistance levels and set stop-loss orders to manage risk.

Utilize technical indicators such as moving averages, Bollinger Bands, or Relative Strength Index (RSI) to confirm breakout signals and identify overbought or oversold conditions.

Momentum Indicators

Momentum indicators can help identify meme coins with strong upward momentum or trend acceleration. Utilize indicators such as the Moving Average

Convergence Divergence (MACD), Stochastic Oscillator or Rate of Change (ROC) to gauge momentum strength.

Look for meme coins with bullish momentum signals, such as upward crossover of moving averages, oversold conditions followed by bullish divergence or ROC spikes indicating rapid price acceleration. Enter trades in the direction of momentum and manage risk with stop-loss orders.

News and Catalyst Trading

News and catalyst trading involves capitalizing on market-moving events, news announcements or developments within the meme coin ecosystem. Stay informed about potential catalysts such as project updates, partnerships, exchange listings or celebrity endorsements.

Monitor social media platforms, news outlets and cryptocurrency forums for breaking news and announcements that could impact meme coin prices. Anticipate market reactions and enter trades ahead of or immediately following significant news events.

Exercise caution and conduct thorough research to validate the authenticity and potential impact of news catalysts. Beware of market manipulation and false rumors that could lead to short-lived price spikes or pump-and-dump schemes.

Scalping and Short-Term Trading

Scalping involves taking advantage of short-term price fluctuations and market inefficiencies to capture small profits. Utilize techniques such as quick entries and exits, tight stop-loss orders, and high-frequency trading to capitalize on short-term momentum. Focus on meme coins with high liquidity, tight bid-ask spreads, and rapid price movements conducive to scalping strategies. Execute trades based on technical analysis, market depth and order flow dynamics.

Monitor market sentiment, news flow, and intraday price action to identify short-term trading opportunities and adapt your strategy accordingly.

By implementing these strategies, meme coin traders can effectively ride momentum, capitalize on price fluctuations and maximize trading profits in the dynamic and volatile cryptocurrency market. Remember to manage risk carefully, set realistic profit targets and remain disciplined in your trading approach.

CHAPTER 9

THE DARK SIDE OF MEME COIN TRADING

Beware of the Memes!

Image used solely for illustration purpose only!

Certainly, meme coin trading, like any other form of investment, comes with its own set of pitfalls, scams and risks. Here are some common pitfalls and scams associated with meme coin trading, along with tips to help readers avoid potential traps and protect their investments.

Pump and Dump Schemes

Risk: Pump and dump schemes involve artificially inflating the price of a meme coin through coordinated buying activity (pumping), followed by selling off large quantities of the coin at inflated prices (dumping) to unsuspecting investors.

Avoidance: Be cautious of meme coins experiencing sudden and unexplained price spikes, especially if accompanied by aggressive marketing tactics or social media hype. Conduct thorough research on the project, team and community before investing to avoid buying into FOMO-driven price rallies without a solid understanding of the fundamentals.

Rug Pulls

Risk: Rug pulls occur when the developers of a meme coin exit the project suddenly, taking with them a significant portion of the liquidity or funds locked in the project's smart contract. This leaves investors holding worthless tokens with no means of recovery.

Avoidance: Perform due diligence on meme coin projects before investing, paying close attention to the transparency and credibility of the development team. Look for projects with locked liquidity or audited smart contracts to reduce the risk of rug pulls. Be wary of anonymous teams or projects with vague whitepapers and unrealistic promises.

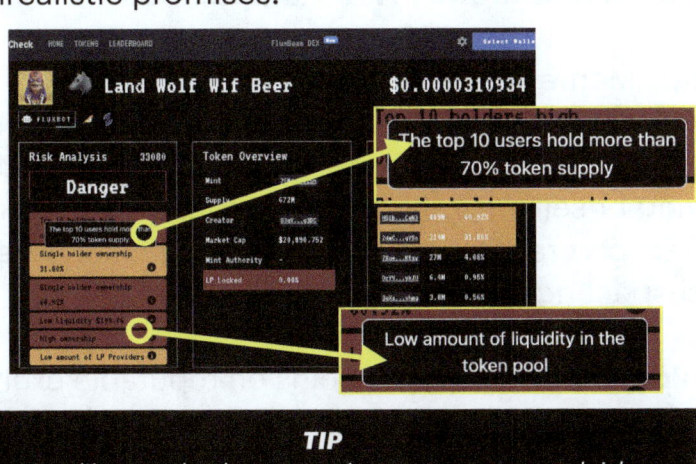

TIP
Sites like rug check.xyz can give you a pretty good risk analysis for some but not all token networks.

Pump Groups and Insider Trading

Risk: Pump groups or "signal" groups operate by coordinating buying activity to artificially inflate the price of a meme coin, often at the expense of unsuspecting retail investors who buy in during the pump. Insider trading involves individuals with advance knowledge of price movements exploiting the information for personal gain.

Avoidance: Exercise caution when joining or participating in pump groups or signal groups promising guaranteed profits. Avoid following tips or signals from anonymous sources without verifying the information independently. Stick to trading strategies based on sound analysis and avoid succumbing to FOMO induced by social media hype.

Illiquid Markets and Price Manipulation

Risk: Meme coin markets with low liquidity are susceptible to price manipulation by whales or large traders, who can influence prices through coordinated buying or selling activity. This can lead to sudden price spikes or crashes, resulting in significant losses for unsuspecting traders.

Avoidance: Trade meme coins on reputable exchanges with sufficient liquidity and volume to reduce the risk of price manipulation. Avoid trading on obscure or unregulated platforms where market manipulation is more prevalent. Use limit orders and avoid market orders to prevent slippage and minimize the impact of price manipulation.

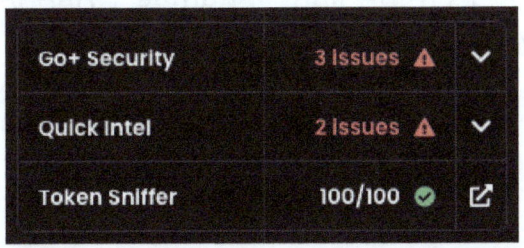

> **TIP**
> *Dex Screener can give you a preliminary "Audit" scan of an index. Alerting you to commonly seen red flags.*

Emotional Trading and Over-leveraging

Risk: Emotional trading, driven by fear, greed, or FOMO, can lead to impulsive decision-making and irrational behavior, resulting in losses. Over-leveraging, or trading with borrowed funds, amplifies the impact of price movements and increases the risk of liquidation in volatile markets.

Avoidance: Develop a disciplined trading strategy based on rational analysis and risk management principles. Set clear entry and exit criteria, along with stop-loss and take-profit levels, to minimize emotional bias and impulsive trading decisions. Avoid over-leveraging and only trade with funds you can afford to lose.

By being aware of these common pitfalls and scams associated with meme coin trading, readers can take proactive steps to protect their investments and avoid falling victim to fraudulent schemes. Conducting thorough research, practicing due diligence, and exercising caution in trading decisions are key to navigating the risks inherent in the meme coin market.

CHAPTER 10

MASTERING MEME COIN TRADING

The Art of the Meme Coin Trader

Becoming a proficient meme coin trader requires a combination of knowledge, skills, and disciplined execution. By synthesizing key concepts, strategies, and insights covered throughout this book, readers can navigate the ever-changing landscape of cryptocurrency with confidence and proficiency. Here's a comprehensive guide to mastering the craft of meme coin trading

What is a Master?

A master is simply one who practices! Practice these steps and techniques and you will be well on your way to mastering Meme Coin and any other trading type, for that matter, in no time!

Lets Recap!

Understand the Fundamentals

Develop a solid understanding of blockchain technology, cryptocurrency fundamentals, and the unique characteristics of meme coins. Educate yourself on key concepts such as supply and demand dynamics, liquidity, market sentiment and risk management principles.

Do your Research and Due Diligence

Conduct thorough research and due diligence before investing in meme coins. Evaluate project fundamentals, team credentials, technology, community engagement, and market potential. Use reliable sources of information and avoid falling victim to hype or scams.

Apply Strong Risk Management

Implement effective risk management strategies to protect your investments and mitigate potential losses. Diversify your portfolio, set stop-loss orders, manage position sizes and avoid emotional trading. Stay disciplined and stick to your trading plan, even in the face of market volatility.

Capitalizing on Opportunities

Identify opportunities for profit by riding meme coin momentum and capitalizing on price fluctuations. Utilize trend following, breakout trading, momentum indicators and news catalysts to enter trades with high profit potential. Stay informed about market developments and adapt your strategy accordingly.

Avoid Pitfalls and Scams

Be aware of common pitfalls and scams associated with meme coin trading, such as pump and dump schemes, rug pulls, insider trading, illiquid markets, and emotional trading. Exercise caution, conduct due diligence, and avoid FOMO-driven decisions.

And Always Continue to Learn and Adapt

Stay informed about evolving market trends, regulatory developments and emerging technologies within the cryptocurrency space. Continuously seek opportunities to learn, adapt, and refine your trading strategies based on new information and market insights.

Stay curious, stay informed, stay disciplined in your strategy and success will follow in this exciting and ever-evolving frontier of finance.

CHAPTER 11

DISPELLING THE MYTH OF "TO THE MOON"

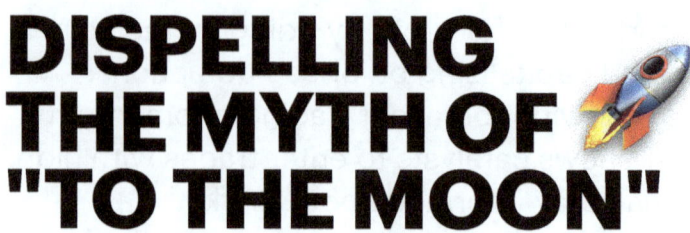

The Art of the Meme Coin Trader

In the world of trading and investing, the phrase "to the moon" has become synonymous with the hope and excitement of witnessing a financial asset skyrocket in value. However, while the idea of exponential growth may be enticing, it's essential to recognize the reality of market dynamics and the likelihood of assets returning to previous support and resistance zones.

Contrary to popular belief, financial assets, whether cryptocurrencies, stocks, or commodities are more likely to adhere to the principles of technical analysis. All exhibit patterns of price movement that are influenced by supply and demand dynamics, market sentiment and investor behavior.

Support and resistance levels play a crucial role in understanding these market dynamics. Support represents a price level at which buying pressure is sufficient to prevent an asset from declining further, while resistance represents a price level at which selling pressure is sufficient to prevent an asset from rising further.

When an asset experiences a significant price increase, it may encounter resistance at previous highs, as traders who bought at lower levels may choose to take profits, creating selling pressure. Similarly, when an asset experiences a price decline, it may find support at previous lows, as buyers may perceive the asset as undervalued and step in to purchase, creating buying pressure.

By understanding the concept of support and resistance, traders can anticipate potential price movements and make informed trading decisions. Instead of blindly chasing dreams of exponential growth, traders can recognize the significance of these key levels and adjust their strategies accordingly.

In essence, while the allure of "to the moon" may captivate the imagination, it's essential to approach trading with a realistic mindset grounded in technical analysis and market fundamentals. By acknowledging the likelihood of assets returning to previous support and resistance zones, traders can navigate the markets with greater precision and confidence. Ultimately, it increases the chances of success in the dynamic world of trading and investing.

EXTRAS

TRADING STATEGIES

MASTER MEME TRADING: REAL WORLD GUIDE TO SUCCESS IN THE CRYPTO MARKET

- **Day Trading:** Day trading involves buying and selling financial assets within the same trading day, with the aim of profiting from short-term price fluctuations.

Traders typically use technical analysis and intraday charts to identify short-term trends and execute trades based on short-term price movements.

Day trading requires constant monitoring of the market and quick decision-making, as positions are typically closed before the end of the trading day.

Benefits: Offers the potential for quick profits and allows traders to take advantage of intraday market volatility. Requires less capital compared to long-term investing.

- **Swing Trading:** Swing trading involves holding positions for several days to weeks, aiming to capture short-to-medium-term price movements within an established trend.

Traders focus on identifying price swings or "swings" within the broader trend and enter positions based on technical analysis and chart patterns.

Swing trading allows for more flexibility compared to day trading, as positions are held for longer durations, but still require active monitoring and management.

Benefits: Provides opportunities to capture larger price movements compared to day trading. Allows traders to take advantage of trends without the need for constant monitoring.

- **Position Trading**: Position trading involves taking long-term positions in financial assets based on fundamental analysis and macroeconomic factors, with the intention of holding them for weeks to months or even years.

Traders focus on identifying assets with strong long-term growth potential and establish positions with the expectation of profiting from sustained price appreciation over time.

Position traders typically have a longer investment horizon and are less concerned with short-term price fluctuations. Instead they focus on the underlying fundamentals of the asset.

Benefits: Allows traders to capitalize on long-term trends and fundamental factors, driving asset prices. It also requires less active monitoring and can be less stressful compared to shorter-term trading strategies.

Scalping: Scalping involves making small profits from frequent trades, typically holding positions for seconds to minutes and aiming to exploit small price movements.

Traders use high-frequency trading techniques and leverage short-term price fluctuations to capture small profits on a large number of trades.

Scalping requires fast execution, tight spreads and low transaction costs to be profitable. It often involves trading high-volume and highly liquid assets.

Benefits: Offers the potential for consistent, albeit small, profits from rapid-fire trading. Can be suitable for traders with a high tolerance for risk and excellent execution skills.

Each trading strategy has its own set of advantages and considerations. The choice of strategy depends on factors such as risk tolerance, time commitment, trading style, and market conditions. By understanding the differences between these strategies, traders can select the approach that best aligns with their goals and preferences.

EXTRAS

LIST OF TRADING TERMS

MASTER MEME TRADING: REAL WORLD GUIDE TO SUCCESS IN THE CRYPTO MARKET

- **Analytical:** Analytical refers to the process of examining and evaluating data, information, and market trends to make informed trading decisions. Traders use analytical tools and techniques, such as technical analysis and fundamental analysis, to assess market conditions and identify trading opportunities.

- **Resistance:** Resistance is a price level at which an asset tends to encounter selling pressure, preventing it from moving higher. Resistance levels are identified on price charts and represent areas where sellers outnumber buyers, causing prices to stall or reverse.

- **Support:** Support is a price level at which an asset tends to encounter buying pressure, preventing it from moving lower. Support levels are identified on price charts and represent areas where buyers outnumber sellers, providing a floor or base for prices to bounce off.

- **Technical Data:** Technical data refers to quantitative information derived from price and volume data of financial assets, such as stocks, currencies, or cryptocurrencies. Technical data includes indicators, oscillators, and other metrics used in technical analysis to analyze market trends, identify patterns, and make trading decisions.

- **Technical Analysis:** Technical analysis is a method of evaluating financial markets and making trading decisions based on the analysis of historical price and volume data. Traders use technical analysis techniques, such as chart patterns, indicators, and trend analysis, to forecast future price movements and identify trading opportunities.

- **Trend Lines:** Trend lines are diagonal lines drawn on price charts to visually represent the direction and strength of a market trend. An uptrend line connects higher lows in an upward trend, while a downtrend line connects lower highs in a downward trend. Trend lines are used in technical analysis to identify trend reversals and potential support or resistance levels.

- **Trends:** Trends refer to the general direction in which the price of a financial asset is moving over time. Trends can be classified as uptrends (rising prices), downtrends (falling prices), or sideways trends (horizontal prices). Traders use trend analysis to identify the direction of the prevailing trend and make trading decisions accordingly.

- **Halving**: Halving refers to a programmed reduction in the rate at which new units of a cryptocurrency are generated or mined. It is a protocol-level event coded into the blockchain that occurs at regular intervals, typically every few years.

- **Mining**: is the process by which new cryptocurrency coins or tokens are created and added to a blockchain network. Miners use powerful computers to solve complex mathematical puzzles, validate transactions, and secure the network by adding new blocks of transactions to the blockchain. In return for their computational efforts and resources, miners are rewarded with newly minted coins or transaction fees.

- **Staking**: is a process in which cryptocurrency holders lock up their coins as collateral to participate in the operation and governance of a blockchain network. Stakers contribute their coins to the network's consensus mechanism, known as proof-of-stake (PoS), and are rewarded with additional coins as incentives for validating transactions and securing the network.

- Yield farming, also known as liquidity mining is a decentralized finance (DeFi) strategy that involves providing liquidity to decentralized exchanges (DEXs) or lending platforms in exchange for rewards or yield. Yield farmers deposit their cryptocurrency assets into liquidity pools, where they are used to facilitate trading or lending activities on DeFi platforms. In return for providing liquidity, yield farmers receive rewards in the form of additional tokens, transaction fees, or interest payments.

Understanding these key terms is essential for traders to conduct effective analysis, identify trading opportunities, and navigate the financial markets successfully. By incorporating these concepts into their trading strategies, traders can enhance their decision-making process and improve their overall trading performance.

Ok, now that we got all of that out the way. Let me show you how I currently use this information and how I have applied it previously in real life.

MY PERSONAL JOURNEY

PUTTING IT ALL TOGETHER

Strategies & Things I've Learned...

Quick back story...like most new traders, I began in commodities. I started with purchasing a few stocks here and there, in the hopes of striking it rich. However, owning just a few shares of a company made it highly unlikely for any substantial profits to materialize. Even if my modest shares did show any significant price movement, any profit was quickly eroded by commissions or broker fees!

One night in the early 2000s, while lying on the couch battling the flu, I stumbled upon this infomercial about the Foreign Exchange Market (FOREX). Instantly, I was hooked! Firstly, because it was something I'd never heard of, and secondly, because it was 3 am. That cold medicine had me float'n in space!

Forex trading involves the buying and selling of currencies in the foreign exchange market. It is the largest and most liquid financial market in the world!

Currencies are traded 24 hours a day, five days a week! I had to learn it.

Sometime later after a lot of research and scrutinizing chart after chart, for what seemed like days on end. Studying for hours at time or until my eyes were swoll! Slowly the patterns of price actions started to become clear, and it was game on!

While most traders searched for that one currency pair to take off, I began to see the repeated movements that happened throughout a day with all pairs. Sometimes they might reach new heights or new lows depending on the trend. Most days however, they'ed just bounce back and forth within a range. Larger time frames would confirm the trend and short ones gave ideas for entry. Once you learn the nuance of a pair and understand market cycles, its not at all as intimating.

I found a broker in the UK that offered an extremely high leverage ratio. I'm talking 1:500! This amount of leverage allowed me to control a large amount of money with a small amount of capital. Within weeks, I was making enough to feel comfortable in submitting my letter of resignation as a Corporate Web Development Manager and begin trading full-time. While the market became predictable to an extent, life on the other hand did not! Just as quickly as things can go up, the descent can be even faster. This turned out to be a very valuable lesson! Not only in life but also in mastering trading market movements, but I will delve deeper into that a little later. In this case, in 2010, the Commodity Futures Trading Commission (CFTC), which is the regulatory body responsible for overseeing the forex market in the United States, decided to implement regulations.

NOTE: *We discussed the importance of **Regulations** in Chapter 5's **Evaluate Market Dynamics** in the **Risk Assessment** section.*

They limited the maximum leverage that brokers could offer to US clients from 1:500 to 1:50 for major currency pairs and 1:20 for minor currency pairs.

Sadly, this was also on the tail-end of the housing bubble of 2008. For many years prior I'd been comfortable carrying two mortgages. Especially while trading at a 1:500 leverage ratio and enjoyed the low pip spread offered by overseas brokers. But now, with this 1:50 or sometimes 1:20 leverage and high pip spreads of US-based brokers added with the collapsing housing market, things proceeded to go downhill quickly. But under all the emotion there was a bigger lesson in this also.

Lets revisit the idea of a rocket launch to the moon. We have a vessel and a target but what does it take to get there? First of all its gonna need fuel to propel it up but what happens when that fuel runs out? It falls back down. This housing market was fueled by low-interest rates, deregulation, over leveraging and FOMO, which caused the housing prices to rise rapidly. Once the market prices got higher other people started to see the effects it had on their property value and wanted in! The only way to benefit is to sell or lets say take profit. Because until then that value was just unrealized gain. It's not profit until it's sold. Knowing this will be very valuable when understanding the Meme market mentality but back to the housing market.

Eventually the market became filled with inventory that was overbought and overvalued. New buyers trying to come in were priced out and what happened when they couldn't afford to continue to fuel the upward momentum? The market crashed and like the rocket it fell back down.

So, now back to trading. Identifying and using overbought and oversold conditions as indicators is nothing new. But I want you to look at it from another perspective that has the potential to take your Meme Coin trading to the next level. In FOREX and other markets you have price history. You can scroll back on charts and view them in multiple time frames with data from 1s to 5 years or more. With cryptocurrencies, especially Meme Coins, most projects are weeks, months, or sometimes even just days old!

So how do we use this to our advantage? First, instead of focusing on price action—or until we get some serious price history—switch your chart from viewing price to viewing Market Cap.

Market capitalization, often referred to as Market Cap, is a measure of the total value of a cryptocurrency, stock, or asset in the market. Calculated by multiplying the current price of the asset by the total number of outstanding units or shares.

In meme coin trading, market cap can sometimes be more important than price for several reasons. Here's a list of how both a high or a low market cap can effect a coin.

GOOD

- Larger market cap is typically considered more established and may have greater liquidity & stability.

- Meme coins with higher market caps are often perceived as more resilient to market fluctuations.

- Larger market cap may offer greater investment opportunities and potential for significant gains.

- Meme coins with higher market caps tend to have greater liquidity, making it easier for traders to execute large orders without impacting the market price.

- A meme coin with a large market cap is often perceived as more legitimate, credible, and trustworthy.

BAD

- Meme coins with low market caps may lack transparency regarding their development team, project roadmap, and underlying technology.

- Meme coins with low market caps are particularly susceptible to pump and dump schemes. Where the price of the coin is artificially inflated by coordinated buying activity, followed by a rapid sell-off.

- Low market cap meme coins often have thin liquidity, meaning there are relatively few buyers and sellers in the market. This can result in wide bid-ask spreads, increased volatility, and difficulty in executing trades at desired prices.

- Meme coins with low market caps may lack an active and engaged community of supporters and investors.

- Meme coins with low market caps may lack a clear use case or value proposition, relying solely on hype or speculation to drive price action.

OK, so now what?

Lets Find Something to Trade

Remember the first steps to finding a good coin is doing our research checking social media platforms, online forums etc. Make sure to checkout the coins personal website, white paper and project roadmap, if it is available. As stated earlier, the lack of transparency is a huge red flag! Don't forget, be cautious of projects that are not forthcoming about their team members, project goals, or future plans. This is essential for mitigating losses and making informed trading decisions.

Ok, you found a solid new project with a good following. Lets look at a couple strategies. Lets Start with **Day Trading**

Identify Key Support and Resistance Levels:

- Start by identifying significant support and resistance levels on the price chart of the meme coin you're trading. These levels can be determined using historical price data, previous highs and lows, or key psychological levels.

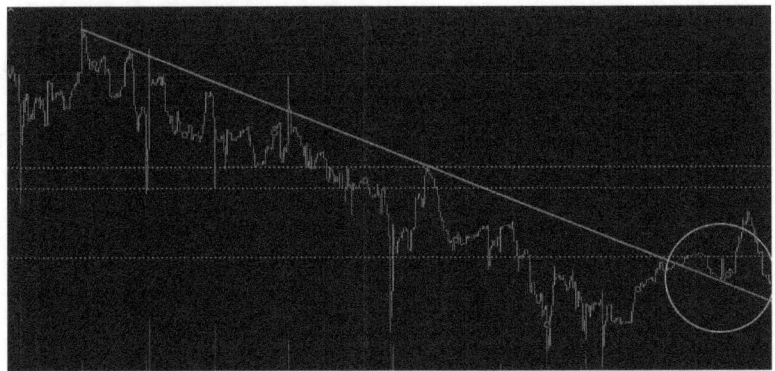

In the chart above the blue trend line is indicating a downward trend. Now the orange circle shows where the price candlesticks broke through the downward trend line. This is potentially indicating a upside reversal.

- Support levels are price levels where buying interest is expected to be strong enough to prevent further price declines. While resistance levels are price levels where selling pressure is expected to be strong enough to prevent further price increases.

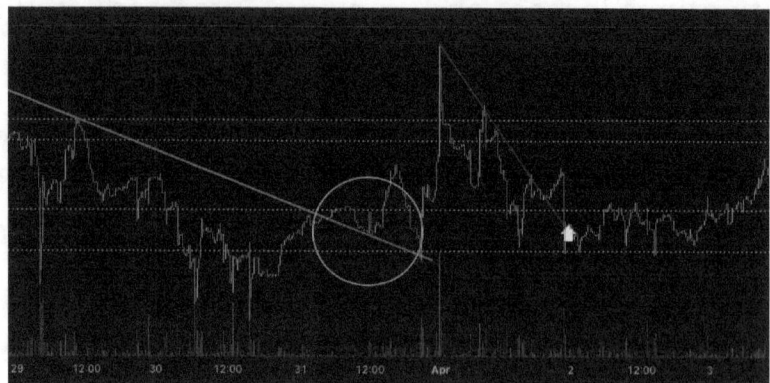

The dotted blue lines show the support and resistance. Look how the price moves between these zones. These bounces can give us buy and sell opportunities.

Confirm Market Cap or Previous Price Zones:

- Determine the meme coin's known market cap or previous price zones that have acted as significant support or resistance levels in the past. These zones can serve as additional reference points for potential price targets or areas of interest.

Wait for Price Action Confirmation:

- Monitor the price action of the meme coin as it approaches key support or resistance levels or known market cap or previous price zones.

- Look for confirmation signals such as candlestick patterns, volume spikes, or trend indicators aligning with the identified support or resistance levels to validate the strength of these levels.

Plan Your Entry and Exit Points:

- Plan your entry and exit points based on the identified support and resistance levels or known market cap or previous price zones.

Set Stop-Loss and Take-Profit Levels:

- Place stop-loss orders below support levels or above resistance levels to manage risk and protect your capital in case the trade goes against you.

- Set take-profit targets at levels where you expect the meme coin to encounter significant resistance or support, based on known market cap or previous price zones.

Reminder: Day traders are in it for the profit and it's not profit till its sold!

Manage Your Trades:

- Monitor your trades closely and adjust your stop-loss and take-profit levels as the price of the meme coin evolves.

- Consider scaling in or out of your positions gradually to capitalize on favorable price movements while minimizing risk.

- Stay disciplined and stick to your trading plan, avoiding emotional decision-making and maintaining a rational approach to trading based on objective analysis.

By implementing this simple day trading strategy, based on support and resistance levels and a meme coin's likelihood to target known market cap or previous price zones, you can potentially identify high-probability trading opportunities. This will maximize your chances of success in this volatile market. However, remember to always conduct thorough research. Be sure to manage your risk, and trade responsibly to achieve your trading goals.

Now lets look at a **Long Term Hold** strategy.

Trading and holding meme coins long term can offer several potential benefits for investors who believe in the long-term viability and growth potential of these projects. Here are some of the benefits:

- **Potential for Significant Returns**: Meme coins, especially those with innovative technology, strong community support, and unique value propositions, have the potential to deliver significant returns over the long term. Holding onto meme coins through market cycles and price fluctuations can allow investors to capitalize on future price appreciation, as the project gains traction and adoption.

- **Early Adoption Advantage:** Investing in meme coins early in their development stages can provide investors with an early adoption advantage. By identifying promising projects with disruptive potential, investors can acquire meme coins at lower prices before they become mainstream. By doing so, this potentially maximizes returns as the project grows in popularity and value.

- **Diversification of Portfolio:** Including meme coins in a diversified investment portfolio can help spread risk and enhance overall portfolio performance. Meme coins often have low correlations with traditional asset classes like stocks and bonds. This provides diversification benefits and reduces portfolio volatility.

- **Community Engagement and Governance:** Holding meme coins long term allows investors to actively participate in the project's community and governance processes. Many meme coins have decentralized governance structures that enable token holders to vote on project proposals, upgrades, and other decisions. Giving investors a voice in the direction and development of the project.

- **Potential for Passive Income:** Some meme coins offer opportunities for passive income through staking, yield farming, or participation in liquidity pools. By holding meme coins in designated wallets or providing liquidity to decentralized exchanges, investors can earn rewards or transaction fees, generating passive income streams over time.

- **Exposure to Emerging Trends:** Meme coins often represent emerging trends and innovations in the cryptocurrency space such as decentralized finance (DeFi), non-fungible tokens (NFTs), and blockchain gaming. Holding meme coins long term allows investors to gain exposure to these emerging trends and potentially profit from their growth and adoption in the future.

- **Psychological Benefits:** Holding meme coins long term can provide psychological benefits, such as reduced stress and anxiety associated with short-term trading and market fluctuations. Taking a long-term perspective allows investors to focus on the fundamentals of the project and its potential for long-term success, rather than getting caught up in short-term price movements.

With that in mind, a solid trading approach can be as simple as buying the dips and sell offs. This is a great way to add to an existing position over time. As a matter of fact, lets see if I can explain it better.

Buying the dip, is also known as Cost Averaging. It's a popular strategy among investors looking to capitalize on short-term price declines while maintaining a long-term bullish outlook on a particular asset. The concept of "buying the dip", involves purchasing an asset when its price experiences a temporary decline. This is often triggered by market fluctuations, negative news, or broader market trends. The goal is to accumulate more of the asset at a lower cost. Thereby, reducing the average purchase price over time.

To identify the dip, investors may monitor price charts and technical indicators to identify potential dips or downward price movements. Dips can occur for various reasons, such as market corrections, profit-taking by traders, or external events impacting sentiment.

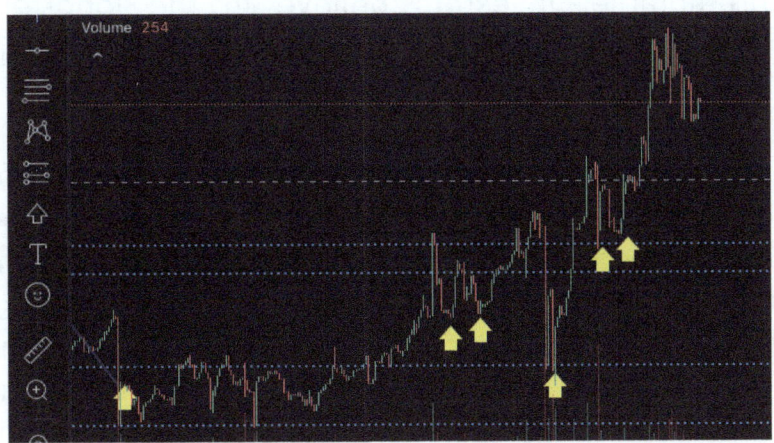

Yellow arrows indicate potential entry points

Investors can implement a cost averaging plan by dividing their desired investment amount into smaller portions and purchasing at regular intervals, regardless of short-term price fluctuations. For example, an investor may decide to allocate a fixed amount of funds to buy every week or month, regardless of whether the price is up or down.

When a dip occurs, investors following the cost averaging strategy will continue to purchase according to their predetermined schedule. By buying more at lower prices during dips, investors effectively lower their average purchase price over time.

It's important for investors to maintain a long-term perspective when implementing the cost averaging strategy. While short-term price fluctuations can be unpredictable, investors believe in the long-term potential of a cryptocurrency with a strong community and widespread adoption.

While buying the dip can be an effective strategy for accumulating assets at lower prices, it's essential for investors to consider the risks involved. Meme coins, like any other cryptocurrency, is subject to market volatility, regulatory uncertainty, and other factors that can impact its price. Additionally, investors should ensure they have a well-diversified portfolio and only invest funds they can afford to lose.

In summary, buying the dip using the cost averaging strategy can be a prudent approach for investors interested in accumulating Crypto coins, while managing short-term price volatility. By purchasing at regular intervals, investors can potentially lower their average purchase price over time and benefit from a cryptocurrency with long-term growth potential.

This can be combined with staking and pooling as mentioned earlier, to potentially further increase the quantity of your holdings.

Even though this is a Long Term Strategy the word "long" can be subjective. It could be as simple as, just more than a day or maybe up to a few years or more. You have to use your best judgement.

For example, in 2020 right at the beginning of the pandemic, my sister would purchase a ton of Kirkland products. Prior to covid, she had a completely different buying habit. With some quick research I found and article saying Costco in-store sales were through the roof, with online orders being up 125%. Another quick google and I discovered the stock price was sub one dollar! This stock peaked at $30 before settling back to normal levels!

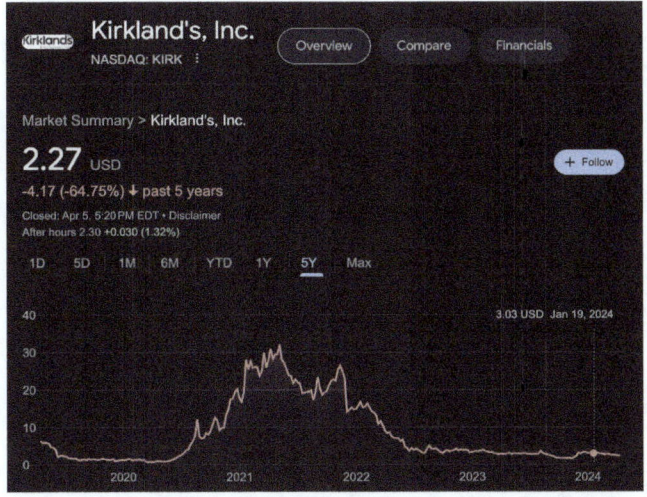

I didn't ride the whole wave but definitely was able to increase my investment by 7-8X. Use wise judgement, stay abreast of news or events related to the project you invested in and always make sure to have an exit plan.

NOTES

NOTES

NOTES

NOTES

NOTES

NOTES

NOTES

NOTES

CONCLUSION

MASTER MEME TRADING

REAL WORLD GUIDE
TO SUCCESS IN THE CRYPTO MARKET

As we conclude this journey into the world of meme coin trading, I hope you have found valuable insights, strategies, and guidance to empower you on your path to mastering this exciting craft. From understanding the fundamentals of blockchain technology to navigating meme coin exchanges and managing risk. We have explored the essential principles and techniques necessary for success in the dynamic and ever-changing landscape of cryptocurrency trading.

Remember that mastering meme coin trading is not just about chasing quick profits or following trends; it's about developing a disciplined approach, informed decision-making, and continuous learning. By applying the knowledge and strategies shared in this book, you can navigate the highs and lows of meme coin markets with confidence. It'll also help to protect your investments, and seize opportunities for profit.

GLOSSARY

MASTER MEME TRADING

1. **Blockchain**: A decentralized, distributed ledger technology that records transactions across multiple computers in a tamper-resistant and transparent manner.

2. **Breakout Trading**: A trading strategy that involves entering positions when the price of an asset breaks out of a key level of support or resistance, signaling a potential shift in market momentum.

3. **Cryptocurrency**: Digital or virtual currencies secured by cryptography and based on blockchain technology, such as Bitcoin, Ethereum, and meme coins.

4. **FOMO** (Fear of Missing Out): The fear of missing out on potential profits or opportunities, leading to impulsive decision-making and irrational behavior in trading or investing.

5. **Liquidity**: The degree to which an asset or security can be quickly bought or sold in the market without significantly affecting its price.

6. **Market Sentiment**: The collective attitude or opinion of traders and investors towards a particular asset or market, often influencing buying and selling behavior.

7. **Market Volatility**: The degree of variation or fluctuations in the price of an asset, reflecting uncertainty and risk in the market.

8. **Momentum Indicators**: Technical indicators used to gauge the strength and direction of market momentum, helping traders identify potential entry and exit points.

9. **Meme Coin**: A type of cryptocurrency that is based on internet memes, cultural references, or jokes, often created as a parody or for entertainment purposes.

10. **Pump and Dump Scheme**: A fraudulent scheme involving artificially inflating the price of an asset (pumping) through coordinated buying activity, followed by selling off large quantities of the asset at inflated prices (dumping).

11. **Regulatory Compliance**: Adherence to laws, regulations, and guidelines governing cryptocurrency trading and investing, aimed at ensuring legal compliance and investor protection.

12. **Risk Management**: The process of identifying, assessing, and mitigating risks associated with

trading or investing, aimed at preserving capital and maximizing returns.

13. **Rug Pull**: A scam where the developers of a cryptocurrency project suddenly abandon the project or exit with a significant portion of the funds locked in the project's smart contract, leaving investors with worthless tokens.

14. **Scalping**: A trading strategy that involves making small profits from frequent trades, taking advantage of short-term price fluctuations and market inefficiencies.

15. **Stop-Loss Order**: An order placed by a trader to automatically sell a security when it reaches a predetermined price level, aimed at limiting potential losses.

16. **Supply and Demand Dynamics**: The relationship between the availability (supply) and desire (demand) for a particular asset, influencing its price in the market.

17. **Take-Profit Target**: A predetermined price level at which a trader plans to sell a security to lock in profits, based on their trading strategy and profit objectives.

18. **Trend Following**: A trading strategy that involves identifying and trading in the direction of established market trends, aiming to profit from the continuation of existing price movements.

REAL WORLD GUIDE TO SUCCESS
IN THE CRYPTO MARKET

MASTER
MEME TRADING

HOW NOT TO GET
SCAMMED!

ADDITIONAL RESOURCES

Binance   https://www.binance.us

Binance is one of the largest and most popular cryptocurrency exchanges globally, offering a wide range of trading pairs.

CoinBase   https://www.coinbase.com

Coinbase is a user-friendly platform known for its ease of use and trusted reputation. It offers a variety of cryptocurrencies for trading, as well as educational content.

Kraken   https://www.kraken.com

Kraken is a well-established cryptocurrency exchange that provides a secure trading environment, advanced trading tools, and a wide selection of cryptocurrencies.

TradingView   https://www.tradingview.com

TradingView is a social network, charting and analysis platform for trader's allowing them to interact and share ideas as well as trade directly in the platform.

DexScreener   https://dexscreener.com

DEX Screener is a DeFi analytics platform that allows users to track activity on decentralized cryptocurrency exchanges across a large number of blockchain networks

CoinMarketCap   https://coinmarketcap.com

CoinMarketCap is a leading cryptocurrency data provider that offers real-time market data, price tracking, and comprehensive cryptocurrency research tools.

CoinGecko.com   https://www.coingecko.com

CoinGecko is another popular cryptocurrency data aggregator that provides in-depth market analysis, price tracking, and comprehensive metrics for thousands of cryptocurrencies.

CryptoCompare   https://www.cryptocompare.com

CryptoCompare is a cryptocurrency data platform offering real-time prices, market analysis, and portfolio tracking tools.

Reddit   https://www.kraken.com

Reddit hosts various cryptocurrency communities (subreddits) where users can discuss trading strategies, share market insights, and engage with other crypto enthusiasts.

X or Twitter   https://www.twitter.com

Many prominent figures known as crypto influencers, share market analysis, trading tips, and insights on Twitter. Following reputable crypto influencers can provide valuable information and insights into the crypto market.

ABOUT THE AUTHOR

COREY RUFFIN

MADE IN THE IMAGE OF THE CREATOR, SO I CREATE...

A little over 14 years ago in my mid 30s, I found the FOREX market and it's been one heck of a ride! Full of ups and downs but the knowledge I've gained on the way has allowed me the freedom to take chances and experience the most I can out of life. I was blessed to leave a comfortable corporate position as Web Development Manager for a famous hair care company and I haven't looked back!

Currently, I work in post production on some of your favorite reality shows on a popular American cable network. Still trading and investing! Just thought I'd share some of the information I've learned along the way.

HALLELUYAH

I want to express my sincere gratitude to everyone who has purchased and read this book. Your support and interest in mastering meme coin trading is greatly appreciated. I hope that the insights and strategies presented here will serve as valuable tools in your journey towards financial success and empowerment in the cryptocurrency space.

Final Disclaimer:

While every effort has been made to provide accurate and reliable information, the content of this book is for educational and informational purposes only. The author and publisher are not financial advisors, and the strategies and techniques presented in this book are not guaranteed to result in profits or investment success.

Cryptocurrency trading carries inherent risks, including the risk of loss of capital, and readers should conduct their own research and seek professional advice before making investment decisions. The author and publisher disclaim any liability for any loss or damage resulting from reliance on the information provided in this book.

All crypto asset branded images used in this guide do not belong to Master Meme Trading and are solely for illustrative purpose only!

MASTER MEME TRADING
REAL WORLD GUIDE TO SUCCESS IN THE CRYPTO MARKET

© 2024 Corey Ruffin. All Rights Reserved.

www.ingramcontent.com/pod-product-compliance
Lightning Source LLC
Chambersburg PA
CBHW070346230526
45471CB00006B/2440